BIOGRAPHY OF VENUS LACY

BEING DIFFERENT

CONQUERING THE ODDS

LAQUAN "LQ" STALLWORTH

BIOGRAPHY OF VENUS LACY

DEDICATION

To my family, friends, coaches, mentors, and fans—your unwavering support has been the foundation of my journey. Through every trial, triumph, and challenge, your encouragement, wisdom, and belief in me have shaped the person I am today. I am forever grateful for the lessons each of you have taught me, the strength you've given me, and the love that continues to carry me.

To my readers—thank you for picking up this book and allowing my story to become part of your world. Every page in this book is filled with the passion, struggles, hopes, and dreams that have defined my path, and I hope something within these words resonates with you. Your willingness to walk this journey with me is a gift I do not take for granted.

To LaQuan (author), thank you for capturing my story and bringing it to life. You have been a dear friend for many years, someone I can confide in without fear of judgment—only encouragement. Thank you for being part of my life and always bringing out the light in every situation.

For those who find a piece of themselves within these chapters, know this—you are not alone. May these words bring courage under challenging moments, happiness when doubt creeps in, and love when you need it most. This book is for you, and I hope it leaves a lasting imprint on your heart.

Your encouragement and love have shaped who I am. Thank you for walking this journey with me

– VENUS LACY

TABLE OF CONTENTS

VENUS LACY

FOREWORD

Greatness is rarely born from ease or comfort. It is forged in the fires of adversity—through trials that test the human spirit and stretch the boundaries of what is possible. The story of Venus Lacy is one of resilience, determination, and an unwavering refusal to accept limits.

Venus's journey isn't just about basketball—it's about overcoming obstacles that would have stopped many in their tracks. Born with her knees turned backward, many doctors doubted Venus would ever walk or run. Despite these daunting predictions, she refused to accept limitations. Through perseverance, faith, and the unwavering support of her family, Venus defied expectations and chased her dreams-dreams that once seemed impossible.

Venus's journey was not a straight path. Growing up in a household with contrasting parental influences, she faced societal and personal challenges that often told her what she couldn't do. Instead of accepting these limitations, she viewed them as obstacles to overcome. Her relentless determination led her to dominate on the basketball court, winning championships at every level and ultimately standing atop the Olympic podium with a gold medal.

Venus's story is powerful because it transcends sports. Her life is a testament to the truth that greatness is not only about talent but also about heart, discipline, and the courage to rise in adversity. She teaches us that struggles do not define us; our response to them does.

This book is more than a biography—it is a source of inspiration. Whether you're an athlete, a dreamer, or someone fighting your own battles, Venus's story will remind you that no obstacle is too great to overcome. It is a story of triumph, silencing doubt, and writing your destiny.

Let this book stand as a reminder: true success belongs to those who refuse to give up. Venus Lacy's journey is living proof of that.

PREFACE

Every so often, a story emerges that transcends sports—pushing beyond the boundaries of competition and statistics to reveal a deeply human journey of perseverance, adversity, and triumph. This is the story of Venus Lacy, a woman whose life was shaped by trials and tribulations but refused to let her circumstances define her.

From an early age, Venus faced challenges that could have easily discouraged her spirit. Yet through her family's dedication, the support of friends, ongoing therapy, and her unwavering determination, she overcame that first major obstacle, the beginning of many battles she would fight throughout her life.

Raised in a large family under strict rules and conflicting parental influences, Venus's upbringing was anything but conventional. Her father held firm beliefs in traditional gender roles, while her mother instilled in her love, strength, and resilience. From this contrast, Venus learned that strength takes many forms. Despite financial hardship, personal loss, and the weight of societal expectations, she

3

carved her own path—proving that limitations only hold power when we accept them.

By adolescence, Venus had already endured adversity beyond her physical challenges. She was bullied, called ugly, dumb, and many other names—simply because she was different. But her mother's unwavering love reminded her she was special. Her mother would tell her that her father had seen something radiant in her that others could not see.

Venus's basketball career exemplifies her unwavering spirit. Despite going undrafted, she refused to give up. She faced countless setbacks, yet her determination never wavered. Through relentless effort, she fought her way into the WNBA, dominated the paint, and eventually earned her place among the world's greatest athletes as an Olympic gold medalist. But beyond the accolades, her story is one of resilience—of finding light in the darkest moments and pushing past the "cant's" to achieve the impossible.

This book is about basketball and the relentless pursuit of greatness in the face of adversity. It speaks to anyone who said that they weren't good, strong, or capable enough. It is a testament to the power of perseverance, the strength of self, belief, and the courage it takes to be different.

Prepare to embark on a journey through the extraordinary life of Venus Lacy—a life that proves success isn't just about talent but heart, determination, and the resilience to rise above all odds.

This book chronicles Venus's journey—its highs and lows, victories and heartbreaks. It is more than a sports story; it is a story of empowerment and the indomitable human spirit. Whether you are an athlete, a dreamer, or someone fighting your own battles, may Venus Lacy's story remind you that with heart and perseverance, no obstacle is too great.

By LaQuan "LQ" Stallworth

INTRODUCTION

In this biography, we take a deep dive into the remarkable life and career of Venus Lacy—a woman whose journey is defined by trials, tribulations, resilience, and triumph. Venus's story is more than a tale of basketball success; it is a powerful testament to the strength of determination, the courage to overcome adversity, and the impact of breaking barriers.

This is not just a sports story. It is an epic narrative about how perseverance and an unyielding spirit can defy all odds. From the beginning, Venus's life was shaped by challenges, yet she refused to let her circumstances define her. Instead, she forged her path, meeting each obstacle with bravery and resolve.

Venus shows us that success is not solely about talent but the will to keep going when the world tells you to quit. She demonstrates that true strength lies in standing tall through adversity and pressing forward. This book goes beyond recounting Venus's accomplishments on the court; it reveals the woman behind the accolades. It explores how she found empowerment through hardship, endured when others might have given up, and chose to embrace her uniqueness rather than hide it. It is, above all, a story of the courage to be different.

Join us on an intimate journey through the life of Venus Lacy—a story that begins in leg braces and rises to Olympic gold through hardship, healing, and purpose. Together, we will explore her formative years in Chattanooga, her rise to basketball stardom at Louisiana Tech, her shining moment on the Olympic podium, and the unforeseen challenges that nearly broke her spirit. We will also witness how she reinvented herself after the cheers faded—emerging as a mentor and a beacon of hope for others. This journey reveals not just what Venus accomplished but how she endured, how she found light in her darkest moments, and how she summoned strength when she felt her weakest.

By the end of this story, you will see Venus Lacy as more than an athlete. You will come to know her as a survivor, a champion of the human spirit, and a woman who discovered a purpose greater than basketball. Let us embark on this incredible journey together—and, in doing so, find inspiration for our own lives. Venus's life is a powerful reminder that the strongest metal is forged in the hottest fire. Her legacy encourages us to face our challenges with the same grit and grace that she has shown throughout her extraordinary life.

As we move through the highs and lows of her story, we'll encounter moments of joy, heartbreak, struggle, and triumph. Hers is a story of unwavering determination—proof that success is not solely about talent but the will to push forward when the world tells you otherwise.

WHO IS VENUS LACY

Let us take an inspiring journey through the life of Venus Lacy. Venus Lacy is a former American basketball star who soared to the pinnacle of success at every game level. A broad, shouldered, muscular 6- foot-4 center, she was a commanding force in the paint during her prime.

Venus Lacy was born and raised in Chattanooga, Tennessee. From a young age, she demonstrated exceptional talent and determination, claiming championships in high school, college, and international levels-including Olympic gold. Known for her dominance in the paint, relentless rebounding, and commanding presence, Venus earned respect from teammates and coaches- not just for her physical power but for her heart, drive, and unwavering perseverance.

Yet Venus Lacy's identity is far beyond her basketball accolades. She is a daughter, a mother, a mentor, and a survivor. She is a woman who has endured personal hardships rarely visible beneath the bright glare of the spotlight. Injuries—and a devastating car accident—cut her professional basketball career short but also opened the door to a different kind of journey: one of self, discovery, healing, and deeper purpose. In the years following the final buzzer of her playing days, Venus confronted and overcame depression, mental health struggles, and personal tragedy. In doing so, she transformed from a sports icon into a symbol of resilience and hope.

Venus Lacy's life story reads like a gripping novel: a humble beginning in the segregated South, a meteoric rise to the peak of athletic glory, a harrowing fall into darkness, and a courageous climb back to discover meaning beyond the game. Today, Venus's legacy is not defined solely by the points she scored or the records she set but by the lives she has touched and the inspiration she continues to offer. This biography explores Venus Lacy at every stage of her journey—from athlete, champion, and fighter to guiding light.

Her voyage is far from over; Venus's story reveals a history of "cant's" met with "shall dos." She kept pushing forward through every turn, twist, and curveball that tried to limit her path. This is more than a timeline of wins and losses— it is a quest to overcome adversity in pursuit of greatness.

EARLY LIFE

Venus Lacy was born on February 9, 1967, on the west side of Chattanooga, Tennessee. She was the eighth of ten children born to Scott Lacy Jr. and Dorothy Lacy. Her father stood about 5'9", while her mother, a graceful and commanding presence, was 5'11". Together, they were a striking couple. Despite the challenges of raising a large family, her parents provided for all ten children and enforced strict household rules.

Scott held firmly to old-fashioned values—he didn't believe women should do "manly" things, like driving, and taught his daughters to serve men while urging the boys to grow into providers. Dorothy, however, stood in quiet contrast. She taught her children to love, to show softness when needed, and to carry strength with compassion. Venus's story grows more layered from here, marked by a childhood filled with contradictions and hardship.

Lacy grew up in an unstable household shaped by joyful moments and violent disruptions. Her father, Scott Jr., eventually abandoned the family when Venus was in ninth grade, following infidelities outside his marriage. His absence left Dorothy to raise the children on her own. Though she struggled—battling financial strain and gambling issues; the disability checks helped keep food on the table and the family afloat.

Growing up in an environment marked by domestic violence is a profoundly challenging and painful experience. For a child, witnessing turmoil between parents leaves lasting scars on both the heart and mind. Venus was caught in the crossfire—not only watching her parents clash but also witnessing her siblings fight while struggling with her own silent battles.

The home, which should have been a place of safety and comfort, became a battleground filled with fear and uncertainty. Venus endured constant arguments, physical altercations, and emotional abuse, all of which created a toxic and unpredictable atmosphere.

Such an environment often leads to long-term psychological effects, including anxiety, depression, and difficulty trusting others. Yet despite these hardships, the fact that Venus grew up surrounded by domestic violence only underscores her incredible resilience.

If you or someone you know is experiencing domestic violence, it is crucial to seek help. Resources and organizations are devoted to offering safety, support, and guidance to those in need. You are not alone; there is help and hope.

BIRTH

Venus Lacy's journey began with adversity. Born with a severe knee condition that caused her legs to turn backward, doctors told her parents she would never walk or run like other children. Unable to afford professional therapy, her family relied on love, faith, and determination. Venus spent her early years confined to braces, wearing them day and night—her childhood was shaped by physical limitations and the quiet strength of those who stood by her.

Growing up in a large family, Venus often felt alone. Her differences made her a target for ridicule, even among her siblings, who didn't fully understand her pain. She was bullied, called ugly and dumb, and constantly had to fight to assert her worth. The challenges didn't end at home—she was mocked for her speech difficulties at school.

Struggling to pronounce words that began with S, C, and R, she faced relentless teasing. Her disability, a burden she was born into, became a defining obstacle—one she would spend years learning to overcome.

While other little kids ran freely through the playgrounds of Chattanooga, Venus often sat on the sidelines—watching, waiting, yearning. She longed to chase after her siblings and friends, but the metal braces and aching legs kept her still. During this difficult time, her mother, Dorothy, became her anchor. Each day,

Dorothy and Venus's grandfather massaged her fragile legs, hoping to stimulate growth and strength. They refused to give up on the dream that Venus would one day walk and run like any other child. It was a simple, repeated act of love—one that, over time, made an extraordinary difference.

A moment that shifted Venus's outlook came when her mother told her that her name was special. It had been chosen by her father, who believed she carried something unique inside—something no one else could see. That thought stayed with her. But true inspiration struck when she watched The Wilma Rudolph Story. Witnessing the journey of Wilma Rudolph—a fellow Tennessean, Olympic gold medalist, and a woman who also wore leg braces as a child—filled Venus with hope. She declared, "I want to be like that."

By the time she reached fourth grade, Venus no longer needed braces. Thanks to the unwavering dedication of her mother and grandfather, she had defied the doctors' expectations. She enrolled at Eastdale Elementary, where teachers placed her in a smaller class that offered extra support. There, she first began to understand she could shape her future.

As she grew older, Venus pushed herself to find her passion. She tried her hand at several sports—softball, cheerleading, and volleyball but none seemed to fit. Then, in ninth grade at Dalewood Junior High, everything changed. That's when Venus discovered basketball. It wasn't love at first sight; she didn't wake up knowing this was her destiny. She had stumbled in other sports, experienced setbacks, and failed. But basketball? This felt different.

Venus was six feet one inch tall when she was introduced to Coach Jennings, who immediately recognized her potential. He trained her relentlessly after school, pushing her to master the fundamentals. Venus embraced the challenge, throwing herself into every drill and lesson. When tryouts came, she stepped onto the court with determination—and made the team.

This was more than just making a roster—it was the start of something bigger. A journey of self-discovery. A chance to prove she was more than the limitations others had placed on her. Venus would always credit her coach and teacher, Francis Elizabeth Donahue, whose unwavering encouragement, quiet, judgment, and free support gave her the space to believe in herself.

Through basketball, Venus found more than just a sport—belonging, love, and the beginnings of true friendship. This was her path. This was her beginning.

THE START

Around this time, Venus found a coach and mentor in Coach Jennings—a man deeply committed to helping her reach a potential she had never imagined.

Starting basketball was humbling. Venus's height, which many assumed would make her an instant star, didn't automatically translate into skill. During her early practices, she fumbled passes and missed easy shots. Her footwork was unsteady, and her endurance was low. Some of the other girls snickered that the "big girl" wasn't so tough after all. But Coach Jennings saw more than mistakes—he saw promise. He refused to give up on her.

After regular practice, he stayed behind with Venus, working tirelessly on post moves, rebounding, and defense. Each afternoon, as long shadows stretched across the asphalt court, there they were—coach and student—grinding through pivots and layups long after everyone else had gone home.

Venus's determination, shaped by the hardships of her childhood, kicked into high gear. She hated being bad at

18

anything and practiced until her legs felt like jelly. Slowly but surely, the pieces started to fall into place.

She learned to use her height to her advantage: keeping the ball high, turning strongly toward the basket, and timing her jumps for rebounds. She wasn't fast, but she discovered she could be dominant. On defense, she realized that raising her long arms could disrupt almost any shot. On offense, she found that no one could stop her if she gained the correct position near the hoop.

Venus was entering the next chapter—high school—where she took her place as the starting center at Brainerd High School. As her basketball journey progressed, Coach Jennings passed the torch to Coach Jackson, the head coach at Brainerd. With several formative years under the guidance of two key mentors—Coach Jennings and Coach Jackson—Venus quickly became a force to be reckoned with on the high school stage.

Under Coach Jackson's guidance and continued support from Coach Jennings, who remained a close mentor, Venus became a powerhouse at the high school level.

By her junior year, Venus stood an imposing 6'2", and that's when her dominance truly took shape. Alongside her teammates, she began to harness her talent, and the spark of something extraordinary started to shine. This period marked a meaningful turning point in her life.

In 1984 Venus led Brainerd High School in Chattanooga, Tennessee, to a state championship. She credits her efforts and the commitment of the entire team and coaching staff for this success. It was a defining chapter that helped shape her future in sports and her confidence off the court.

A young Venus was forced by passion, molded by hardship, and destined for something greater. By her senior year, she grew taller, drawing the attention of college recruiters nationwide. In 1985, Venus was honored as Miss Basketball during her final season after completing her standout prep career at Brainerd High School in Chattanooga, Tennessee.

Despite being recruited by powerhouse programs like the University of Tennessee and UT Chattanooga, Venus chose to sign with Old Dominion University. When asked why she turned down schools closer to home, she explained that she needed distance—from the place where she was bullied, laughed at, and burdened by painful memories. She had never left Tennessee before; this was her chance to experience life beyond what she had known. Growing up in a Black neighborhood, this move was her way of preparing for the larger world and learning to adapt and escape from what she did. But her first season in Norfolk didn't go as she had imagined.

THE JOURNEY

V enus began her first year at Old Dominion as a 6-foot-4 center. She was still learning and adjusting to the elevated level of play. The game's speed, the talent of both teammates and opponents, and the intensity of daily practice hit her hard; it shocked her system. Venus was low on the depth chart, still trying to grasp basic post techniques that veteran players had already mastered.

At the time, one of ODU's fiercest rivals was the Louisiana Tech Lady Techsters. Venus recalls the 1984–85 season as a turning point in her life. Midway through her first year, ODU was set to face the Lady Techsters at "The Old Field House" in Norfolk. It was January 17, 1986, when Louisiana Tech defeated ODU with a score of 77–70. That game marked the first time Coach Leon Barmore saw the tall, young player in action. She didn't log in for many minutes, but Venus still impressed the opposing team. She recorded four points and three rebounds in 18 minutes of play for the Lady Monarchs.

Venus appeared in 25 games during her first year, averaging a modest 3.7 points and 4.7 rebounds. Eventually, she and ODU mutually parted ways as she sought a new path in college basketball. Unhappy and searching for a better fit, Venus considered her options. That's when Louisiana Tech's Head Coach Leon Barmore and Assistant Coach Kim Mulkey caught wind of her situation and brought her to Ruston, LA. Due to NCAA transfer rules, Venus had to sit out the following year, giving Barmore, the coaching staff, and her teammates—especially Teresa Weatherspoon—time to develop her skill set.

In her first year wearing a Lady Techsters uniform, Venus averaged 14.5 points and 9.2 rebounds per game. In Tech's 68–59 national semifinal win over Tennessee, she recorded a double, double with 11 points and 10 rebounds. She followed up with four points and eight boards in the 56–54 victory over Auburn in the championship game. Venus played a key role in helping the Lady Techsters capture the 1988 national title.

By the time Venus reached her junior and senior seasons, she averaged 22.7 points and 12.3 rebounds across her final two years in Ruston, leading the Lady Techsters to two additional Final Four appearances.

During her junior season, she was part of the most lopsided win in Techsters history. Venus scored 35 points, grabbed 16 rebounds, and dished out four assists in the first half of a 126–25 victory over Texas Pan American at the Thomas Assembly Center on February 18, 1989. Three minutes midway through that first half, Venus knocked down a trio of three-pointers, the only ones of her college career.

Following her senior season, she averaged 24.2 points and 12.7 rebounds per game. This remarkable performance earned Venus a spot as a Kodak All-American, and she was named both the USBWA and Champion National Player of the Year. She finished her Louisiana Tech career with 2,004 points, the fourth highest in program history—and remains the only Tech player to ever average 20.0 points per game over a career.

Venus led Louisiana Tech to three consecutive Final Four appearances, including the 1988 national title. As a senior in 1990, she played a pivotal role in guiding the Lady Techsters through an unbeaten regular season and securing the No. 1 national ranking before a heartbreaking upset by Auburn in the Final Four.

That same year, Venus earned WBCA Player of the Year honors and was recognized as a consensus All-American. She was inducted into the Louisiana Tech Hall of Fame in 2011 and still holds the No. 4 spot on the program's all-time scoring list.

Her dream was to emulate the greatness of Louisiana Tech legends—Janice Lawrence, Pam Kelly, Debra Rodman, Tori Harrison, Erica Westbrook, and Nora Lewis, all in one. Today, in the pages of history, Venus Lacy's name stands proudly among the top centers and forwards ever to wear a Lady Techsters jersey.

She successfully earned her bachelor's degree.

*After such a stellar college career, one might assume Venus Lacy would be a top pick in a professional league. However, in 1990, **no American women's pro basketball league** was in operation—the WNBA had yet to be founded, and the Women's Professional Basketball League had folded back in 1981. Like many standout women athletes of her time, Venus turned to opportunities overseas to launch her professional basketball career.*

NEXT LEVEL

V enus Lacy set her sights on the professional stage. With no American league available then, she took her talents overseas. Her first stop was Japan, where she signed with the Sanyo women's basketball team. There, Venus quickly became a star, earning All-Star honors in both of her two seasons. She showcased the same dominant post-play that had defined her college career. Despite being far from home, she adapted to the culture and style of play, helping her team contend for championships.

One of the first things Venus did after receiving her Japanese contract revealed her character. She wrote a check for $5,000 and sent it back to Louisiana Tech as a donation to the program that had "changed her life." "A lot of people take," she said. "I just wanted to give back to the school that changed my life." It was her way of expressing gratitude to the coaches and university that had given her so much. This generosity earned her even greater respect from her mentors and fans back home.

With no American professional league available after graduation, Venus continued her career overseas, playing in Greece, Italy, and Japan. In 1996, she led her Greek team to victory in the European Club Championship.

While Venus thrived internationally, major developments were underway in the United States. Inspired by the popularity of women's basketball during the 1996 Atlanta Olympics, two professional leagues emerged: **the American Basketball League (ABL) and the Women's National Basketball Association (WNBA)**. ABL launched first in the fall of 1996, positioning itself as a winter league with teams based mostly in midsize markets. Given Venus Lacy's reputation, she quickly became a highly sought-after player for the new league.

In 1996 Venus was selected as the first overall pick in the inaugural ABL Draft, joining the Seattle Reign. However, in February 1997, she was involved in a serious car accident that left her injured and changed her game permanently. The Reign folded after just one year, and the following season, Venus was drafted by the Nashville Noise, an ABL expansion team that played only 15 games before folding. On December 22, 1998, ABL ceased operations entirely.

Venus went undrafted by the WNBA but was later picked up by New York Liberty in early 1999. She played a few games with the team during the 1999 and 2000 seasons, briefly returning to the professional stage she had long awaited.

Venus played with the USA team at the 1991 Pan American Games in Havana, Cuba. The team finished with a 4–2 record and secured the bronze medal. The U.S. lost a close three-point game to Brazil but bounced back with victories over Argentina and Cuba, earning a spot in the medal round. In a rematch with Cuba, the host team prevailed again, this time by five points. The USA then defeated Canada handily to take the bronze. Lacy averaged 9.4 points per game during the tournament.

Venus was also a member of the 1996 Olympic team that won the gold medal. She was the final player added to the USA's 12-woman roster, joining midway through the team's year-long exhibition tour to add size to the paint. During that historic Olympic preparation year, the team went undefeated, 52–0, facing various college teams, all-star squads, and international opponents. Lacy's presence added valuable depth and strength to the roster, contributing to one of the most dominant runs in women's Olympic basketball history.

The Olympic victory was more than just a personal achievement—it marked a turning point for women's basketball in the United States. The success and visibility of the 1996 women's Olympic team ignited national interest in the emerging professional leagues. Venus took immense pride in being part of that influential group, often called the Women's Dream Team, which showed the country that women's basketball could fill arenas and command headlines.

Back in her hometown of Chattanooga, the community swelled with pride. To honor her Olympic accomplishment, the city renamed a portion of a roadway, "Venus Lacy Parkway." Driving down that street and seeing her name on the sign felt surreal. For Venus, it symbolized the journey—from a little girl in leg braces to a hometown hero immortalized in street signs.

Venus later returned to Ruston to give back once more—this time by mentoring a new generation of Lady Techsters. She guided young players like Alisa Burras, LaQuan Stallworth, and others, helping them understand the game and what wearing the Lady Techsters uniform truly meant.

By this point, Venus's legacy in sports was firmly established. She had won titles at every level: a high school state championship, an NCAA national championship, and an Olympic gold medal. Along the way, she earned individual accolades and Hall of Fame honors. These accomplishments brought Venus immense pride—not in a boastful way but in a deeply reflective one. Each trophy and plaque symbolized a chapter in her life, each one hard-earned and meaningful.

Yet even as Venus celebrated these milestones, life was preparing for new challenges. In the same year she was drafted into the ABL and stood atop the Olympic podium, she would soon face an event that would drastically alter the course of her career—and her life.

TRAGEDY

About 18 months later, while playing for the Seattle Reign of the ABL, Venus was involved in a serious car accident. Everything began to shift. Her love for the game started to fade. This was when depression and mental illness began to take hold of her life. She wanted to give up, not just basketball but life itself.

During this dark period, things worsened. Her weight climbed rapidly, reflecting the inner turmoil she could no longer suppress. She tried to express to friends and family that something wasn't right, but back then, mental illness was often brushed aside, something people were simply expected to "get over." The accident had left deep scars, both physical and emotional, triggering memory loss and a debilitating depression that would shadow her in the years that followed.

While battling depression, mental illness, and memory loss, Venus gave birth to her child, Alex. During this time, she also discovered she was experiencing postpartum depression, adding weight to an already overwhelming struggle.

In 2009, Venus faced another devastating loss: her mother, her best friend and self-described rock, passed away.

OFF THE COURT

For all her success, trouble was never far from Venus's life. Behind the accolades and victories lay a story of survival—one shaped by abuse, betrayal, and an unrelenting battle against her own demons.

From childhood, Venus knew suffering. She wasn't just dealing with the typical struggles of growing up; she was a witness to abuse and eventually became a victim herself. That pain carved deep scars into her life.

The torment she endured was unimaginable: black eyes from brutal beatings, days locked in the darkness of a closet, bones broken by the very hands that were supposed to protect her. Even though she dominated on the court, her life off the court was a private nightmare. She learned to be tough, to stand tall like an unbreakable flower—but even the strongest can wilt under relentless cruelty.

Sometimes, Venus had her head smashed in, and in her fragile state of mind, she believed this was "love." The most heartbreaking part was her belief that love meant sacrifice—enduring pain just to hold on to a piece of a man. The brutal beatings didn't just leave bruises on her body; they left wounds on her soul. In the end, the violence took more than just her dignity—it stole a child from her arms.

But the suffering began long before adulthood. In fourth grade, Venus fell prey to a monster, a predator, a sick individual she once trusted. Her own teacher shattered her innocence. Silenced by fear, she bore the weight of that dark secret alone, trapped in a world where trust had been twisted into a weapon.

One of the most dominant figures in women's basketball, Venus Lacy, continued to fight an invisible war long after the final buzzer sounded. Off the court, she spiraled—battling depression, haunted by past trauma, and entangled in a series of legal troubles. Drunk driving arrests, domestic violence incidents, and the unrelenting shadow of mental illness loomed over her life.

The breaking point came when she realized she could no longer fight alone. She needed help. So, she did what she had to do: she checked herself into a mental institution, a desperate and courageous attempt to reclaim the life that had been stolen from her, piece by piece.

Athletes are often seen as invincible, but those who are injured, near retirement or searching for a purpose beyond the game face a hidden battle. For Venus, that battle was loneliness—a deep yearning for love, acceptance, and something real.

On the court, she was fierce and unshakable. But off the court, the emptiness consumed her. She had spent a lifetime chasing unconditional love, only to discover that every love she had ever known came with strings attached, each demanding more than her heart could afford.

THE PRIDE

Seth Alexander "Alex" Lacy was born on November 1, 2002—and he became the love of Venus's life. With his arrival, Venus began to see the world through a new lens. He was perfect, a blessing from God. Becoming a mother gave her the clarity she needed. She knew it was time to walk away from the toxic relationship she had endured for years. She realized that chasing a man had cost her nearly everything she had worked hard to achieve. But this—this child—was different. Having a son gave her the strength to focus on her well-being and raise him in a healthier, safer environment.

There was a time when no one truly knew how lost Venus felt, how trapped she was in a darkness that seemed impossible to escape. Depression had wrapped itself around her, turning every day into a struggle. She could barely see beyond the pain. But everything changed—because of her son. For the first time, in his tiny hands, Venus found hope. In his eyes, she saw a future. He gave her a reason to live. He became the light that pierced through the shadows and broke the hold another person had once had over her.

From that moment on, Venus felt a purpose greater than life itself—a reason to wake up and keep moving forward. The love she had prayed for was now cradled in the body of an innocent child. She found healing, peace, joy, and a renewed sense of faith through him. His laughter became her medicine, hugs for her refuge, and presence the most significant source of calm she had ever known.

He is the reason she refuses to give up, no matter how difficult life becomes. When she feels weak, she looks at him and remembers that she is his foundation, protector, and role model.

To this day, Alex—as we lovingly call him—is her pride and joy. He is everything and makes it his mission to ensure she feels safe and loved. Out of respect for Alex, we won't delve further into their shared life. Just know this: they are each other's rock.

THE RISE, FALL, AND REDEMPTION OF A CHAMPION

Venus Lacy was born with a fire inside her, the kind that transforms ordinary athletes into legends. She trained relentlessly, climbing through high school and college basketball ranks, leaving shattered records and awe in her wake. In those years, moments of triumph gave her glimpses of happiness, creating a life lit, even briefly, by joy.

Venus had become a household name by the time she reached the national stage. She played with a almost divine fury—an unstoppable force of nature. Every game displayed power and grace: slicing through defenses with precision, delivering blocks that sent opponents sprawling, and commanding every inch of the court with her presence.

The pinnacle of her career came when she was selected for the U.S. Olympic team. Under the brightest lights on the world's biggest stage, she soared. She helped lead her team to gold—her name forever etched into the annals of history, a symbol of greatness, resilience, and unshakable will.

COACH LEON BARMORE

COACH JENNINGS /COACH JACKSON

ALEX

THE RISE

The mid,1990s marked the peak of Venus Lacy's athletic career. By 1997, she had reached heights fewer than ever. Fresh off her Olympic triumph, she prepared to launch her professional career with the newly formed ABL's Seattle Reign. At that moment, Venus felt nearly invincible.

Her name was in the headlines, and young girls looked up to her as a role model. She played with fearsome intensity— a true force of nature on the court—swatting away shots and muscling through defenders. Every game became a stage for her brilliance, and she relished the feeling of being at the top. After years of relentless work, she had become, in many's eyes, a real-life Wonder Woman of basketball.

Her professional debut in the ABL was highly anticipated. Seattle fans were thrilled to have an Olympian anchoring their new team. When Venus stepped onto the court for the Reign, it symbolized "the rise"—from a struggling beginner to an elite veteran. Early games showed flashes of her dominance; she quickly became a crowd favorite, known for her high-energy play and the occasional trademark scowl at opponents bold enough to challenge her in the paint.

At the same time, Venus's personal life was also in a good place. For the first time, she felt financially stable, thanks to her overseas earnings. She was engaged with her community and dreamed of using her platform to inspire young people, especially those who, like her, had grown up in hard places and needed to see what was possible.

THE FALL

But soon, the weight of the world grew unbearably. Expectations and pressure fed a relentless cycle of performance that left her gasping for air. Venus had spent her life chasing perfection—but perfection came with a cost.

The depression crept slowly like a shadow flickering at the edge of her vision. She felt numb. Once her refuge, the court transformed into a place of quiet torment.

She tried to push through, as champions were expected to. But no amount of training could calm the storm inside. The joy she once found in the game faded, replaced by anxiety and despair. Her once resilient body began to falter. Injuries took longer to heal, and fatigue arrived sooner. She withdrew, shutting out teammates, friends, and even family.

She sought temporary escapes, drinking, partying—but nothing worked. The deeper she spiraled, the farther salvation seemed. One evening, after yet another match where she barely recognized herself, Venus sat alone in her apartment, staring at her Olympic medal. It felt like a relic from another lifetime.

She was lost.

The end of Venus's playing days marked one of the darkest chapters of her life. Without basketball, she struggled to find meaning. The injuries and setbacks had fueled a spiral of depression that she'd never truly confronted while clinging to the game. Now, with silence replacing the crowd's roar, her demons found her. She felt numb. The sport that had given her structure and identity for two decades was gone. Venus said: "I just wanted to give up. I just wanted to take my life. I did not want to live," she confided, trying to make sense of why such darkness had taken hold.

But depression doesn't care about medals. Inside, Venus felt a crushing emptiness.

THE REDEMPTION

The turning point in Venus Lacy's life came in the early 2000s—slowly at first, then all at once. After hitting rock bottom, a few vital lifelines appeared. One came through the voice of an old coach.

An old coach called and said, "Venus, you don't have to fight this alone."

For the first time, she listened.

She began therapy—uncomfortable at first, uneasy facing pain long buried. Gradually, however, she started to see herself as more than just an athlete. She was a person who had tied her self-worth to performance.

She reconnected with her family and old friends, who reminded her she was loved—regardless of how many points she scored. She began advocating for mental health awareness, openly sharing her journey. Athletes across various sports reached out, confiding their hidden battles.

Eventually, she returned to the game—not as the unstoppable force she once was, but as something greater. She became a coach and mentor to young athletes, teaching the sport and the value of balance, mental health, and self-worth beyond the scoreboard.

One evening, in a packed gym, she watched fresh players take the court—and for the first time in years, she felt peaceful.

Venus Lacy had risen. She had fallen. But in the end, she found something more precious than gold: herself.

Today, Venus describes her journey in simple, powerful words: "I'm stronger than I thought I was," she says. Her redemption wasn't about reclaiming athletic fame but healing and using her story to help others. She now believes that her trials prepared her to inspire and guide those on similar paths. In her own words: "I want to motivate.

I want to inspire young athletes, young women, people. I believe in faith. I believe in God. I believe in myself. I am stronger than I thought I was." That declaration—anchored in faith and self-belief—is the triumph of Venus Lacy's spirit. It proves she didn't just survive the fall; she rose into a new light. A light defined by hope, service, and unbreakable resilience.

DOROTHY LACY

A SUPPORT OF A MOTHER

Achievement in sports is often attributed to an athlete's skill, commitment, and persistence. But behind every great athlete stands a mother—whose sacrifices, encouragement, and unwavering support shape the journey. From early practices to the biggest competitions, a mother is the constant force that nurtures dreams, instills discipline, and offers comfort in moments of doubt. Her role lays the foundation for confidence, resilience, and character.

A mother's support begins long before the world notices an athlete's potential. She rises before dawn to drive to practice, prepares meals that fuel performance, and ensures her child has everything needed to succeed. She watches countless games, whether from the stands or the living room, cheering victories and offering steady words after defeat. She studies the sport, learns the rules, and becomes their loudest fan and fiercest protector. Through every scraped knee, sore muscle, and moment of exhaustion, she's the one who gently reminds them why they started in the first place.

Beyond physical and logistical support, a mother plays a vital role in shaping an athlete's mindset. She instills values of hard work, humility, and perseverance. When uncertainty arises, she offers encouragement, reminding them that obstacles are simply steps on the journey to success. She urges them to push beyond their limits while stressing the importance of balance, mental well-being, and self-care. Many athletes— even at the height of their careers—credit their mother as the reason they never gave up. Her unwavering belief often becomes the foundation of their self-belief.

Even in the middle of a live event, athletes know their greatest supporter has always been their mother. She may not stand on the podium or wear a jersey, but her influence is undeniable. She is the quiet strength during training, the belief in challenging moments, and the heart behind every triumph. Behind every athlete is a mother who always believed—and that alone is a victory.

In honoring Dorothy, Venus also ensures her story is told: the story of a mother's love that knew no bounds. Dorothy Lacy's presence is woven through every chapter of Venus's journey—an invisible hand guiding her daughter toward hope and light. And when Venus is asked where her strength comes from, she often smiles and says, "I got it from my mom."

STILL WRITING MY STORY

Venus Lacy is a living thread in the fabric of women's basketball history, having won championships at every level. Her name resonates not just for her victories but also for her unwavering dedication to the game and her lasting impression as an athlete.

Venus is living proof that limitations are meant to be broken. Once told she'd never walk alone, she defied every odd to become an Olympic gold medalist. Her journey was one of physical endurance and profound mental strength. She endured relentless bullying, ridicule, and abuse in many forms. Yet Venus rose above it all, showing the world that triumph is possible for those who refuse to quit.

Her message is clear: God has the final say. Venus wants you to know that you must never give up on yourself, no matter the odds. Be your biggest fan and believe life holds something meaningful for you.

Today, Venus continues to draw inspiration. She teaches at her former high school, giving back to the community that shaped her—even as her healing journey continues. Venus now spends her time volunteering with nonprofit programs and mentoring young girls who want to learn the game of basketball. She has refused to give up on herself.

This is the story of Venus Lacy: Being Different.

APPRECIATION

I appreciate you for sticking with me this far—it truly means a lot. Putting this project together has been a journey I've genuinely enjoyed. As Venus spoke, I wrote this from a live conversation between us, her telling her story in real-time. I truly enjoyed the process and hope it's been as meaningful for you.

Thank you for taking this break! Now, let's return to the rescheduled program with Venus Lacy.

DEEPER
PART 2

BATTLE

Venus Lacy had always been a fighter—from the moment she couldn't walk to the moment she first stepped onto a basketball court. She learned early that success demanded discipline, an unbreakable will, and relentless determination. That same mindset carried her through years of grueling training, painful injuries, and the pursuit of greatness. By the time she reached the professional level, she had become one of the most respected female athletes in the game. But no amount of training could have prepared her for the toughest battle she would face beyond the court.

ILLUSION

Many women dream of the perfect illusion—meeting the love of their lives and having the perfect marriage. Venus thought she had found that dream. He was supportive, charming, and quick to shower her with affection. He introduced himself as a businessman with a passion for sports and spoke at length about how much he admired strong women. He made Venus feel special in a way no one else ever had. Since childhood, all she had longed for was love. After years of living in the spotlight—constantly scrutinized for every move—he became her escape from it all.

Their love moved fast—too fast. It quickly escalated to the next level. Looking back, Venus would realize how blind she had been to the warning signs: possessiveness, the cheating, the lies, and the manipulation she endured. He subtly tore her down with repeated criticism, making her feel like a rag doll. Then came the sexual abuse—forcing himself on her when she wasn't willing. And when she tried to resist, he retaliated by giving himself to others. Venus had to watch other women with the man she genuinely loved. She remembered sitting helplessly as he made love to other women right in front of her—and how he dared her to react. But at the time, she believed that having a piece of a man was better than having no man at all.

DARKNESS

After being sexually abused by the man you once loved, imagine your life slowly fading. Being hit, punched, and cut down by cruel words that chipped away at your spirit—bit by bit.

At first, she fought back, refusing to let him break her. But the more she resisted, the more explosive his anger became. His behavior became increasingly unpredictable, and she constantly apologized for things beyond her control to keep the peace.

Just imagine coming home from doing your job and the moment you walk through the door—the first slap across your face. She came home exhausted, hoping for comfort. Instead, he was angry, and before she could even speak, his hand struck her face, sending a siren ringing in her ears. He apologized immediately, crying and begging for forgiveness. He swore it would never happen again. And like so many women before her, she believed him.

That was the first time he laid hands on her, but it wasn't the last. It happened again. And again.

TRAPPED

Venus became skilled at hiding her pain and bruises. Sometimes, makeup masked the marks, long-sleeved shirts covered her arms, and knee-high socks concealed the rest. The physical pain was unbearable, but the worst part was the loneliness. It led her to believe that a man who beats a woman must somehow love her. Venus began to isolate herself, cutting off family and friends. He made her think that no one would ever love her the way he did. He stripped away everything in her soul, always finding new ways to make her feel small. Whenever she tried to reach out, he'd convince her that no one would believe her, what if the public found out? And remind her how much she stood to lose if she spoke up.

To make matters worse, there were times when, after being hit, kicked, and spat on, she was forced to sleep in the closet. Those nights left her feeling broken, trapped in a nightmare, confused, and at times questioning her own worth.

Each painful incident sparked a storm of internal conflict for Venus. She wrestled with herself in silence: could her lack of affection have triggered his behavior? The relentless cycle of abuse and self-doubt blurred the line between care and culpability, leaving her to wonder if her love had simply not been enough.

Regaining her lost faith in the Lord became crucial to her journey of self-discovery. It may not happen on your time, but if you allow God to use you, the redefining of life begins.

FINDING THE STRENGTH

The breaking point came after a victory on the road. Seeing how much she meant to the fans and young kids made her realize she was somebody. Speaking to the Lord daily gave her back the strength she thought she had lost. For a moment, she felt like herself again.

But when she returned home, the house was cold, dark, and heavy with tension. The devil himself was waiting.

Venus looked into his eyes, and something inside her shifted. She wasn't going to let him steal this moment from her. She stood tall—and felt a swift rush of air pass right in front of her.

She knew then—she would never let him take anything from her again.

Venus fought back with every inch of her body and every ounce of strength she had. At that moment, she knew she was free. She walked out of that home and never looked back. The process was painful, exhausting, and terrifying—but for the first time, she felt free.

NEW BEGINNING

We briefly touched on Venus seeking help in this book. A crucial part of that journey was healing therapy, which helped her confront years of abuse—from childhood through adulthood. Healing doesn't happen overnight; Venus is still walking through the process.

She's using her platform to advocate for survivors and be a voice for those still trapped in silence.

She had endured the worst—but she survived.

MENTAL

PART 3

Even gold can feel heavy when you carry it alone

THE WEIGHT OF GOLD

Venus spent most of her life chasing greatness—from learning to walk and run to excelling in sports. When she first stepped onto a basketball court as a young girl, she expected more from herself. She trained hard, sacrificing pieces of her childhood to master the game. Over time, she unlocked the beast within—the warrior spirit she was born with. And there she stood, at the top of an Olympic podium—a gold medal around her neck. The national anthem is playing. It was supposed to be the happiest moment of her life.

But when the cheering and roaring faded, the cameras stopped flashing, and she was left alone with her thoughts, Venus felt a sense of emptiness she couldn't explain.

THE FALL

etirement came too soon. Not by choice but by necessity. Injuries, mental health issues, and physical and sexual abuse caused her to lose the love of the game. Do not get it wrong, because it was a time when she stepped on the basketball court and felt that her teammates did not want her. This came during the Olympic tryouts. Only a few, not many, embraced her. However, that is another story.

The moment she announced her retirement, it seemed like everything had changed. The calls, the sponsors, and the fans moved on to the next athlete. Even some of her teammates she once called family drifted away. She watched the world around her no longer exist and had a place for her.

She tried to reach out to others, but they brushed her off at this moment, and nothing could fill the void: the adrenaline, the purpose, or the validation of the game. The gold medal that once defined her felt like a cruel reminder of everything she had lost. And now the dream was over; she had nothing left.

NOT GOOD ENOUGH

The doubt crept in—slowly at first. Venus kept hearing the same words she had heard as a child: You are not good enough. You will never be anybody. You're not special. You were never that great. You were just a moment in time—and you don't matter.

Venus spent hours in bed, staring at the ceiling, wondering who she was without the sport that had once defined her entire existence. She avoided mirrors; the reflection staring back no longer resembled the strong, disciplined athlete she used to be. She began ignoring phone calls, withdrawing from everyone, and disappearing into herself.

And no one seemed to notice.

BREAKING POINT

Venus started drinking to quiet the thoughts. It numbed the pain and dulled the self-doubt. But when she woke each morning, the weight of emptiness remained.

One evening, after drinking too much, she found herself standing on the edge. The thought crept in: What if I just let go? Would anyone even care?

Venus remembered the darkest thoughts—of ending her life—and how a few of her sisters, instead of helping, told her to do just that. She was losing it. She realized she was not okay and couldn't keep pretending otherwise.

With no one to lean on, this was the moment she had to save her own life.

FINDING MY SOUL

This was the moment she had to make the hardest decision of her life. She asked for help. She called a mental institution and admitted the truth to herself. It wasn't an instant fix. There were days she questioned whether she would ever feel whole again.

Venus found her purpose—not in reliving her past but embracing her future. She began mentoring young athletes, helping them navigate the pressures she had once faced. This gave her a chance to openly share her struggles and realize her story could help others. She felt like she belonged for the first time in a long time.

Venus Lacy was more than a gold medalist. She was more than a moment in history.

She was a survivor—and she was enough.

Having journeyed through the epic highs of victory and the depths of personal despair, Venus Lacy has gained a unique perspective on life's deeper meanings. This section explores the insights and lessons she has drawn lessons that reach beyond basketball into the universal human experience.

One of the most profound lessons Venus often shares is about identity. Her self-worth was tightly bound to being a basketball player for a long time. When she could no longer play, she felt lost, unsure of who she was. Through reflection and counseling, she understood the danger of basing one's identity solely on a career or talent. Who am I when the applause stops? Answering that question requires soul searching.

Venus realized that while basketball was something she did exceptionally well, it was not the whole of who she was. She was also a daughter, a sister, a mother, a friend, and a woman of faith. This realization set her free. It meant that her life had purpose and value even without the game. Now, she encourages others to explore their identities beyond their job or sport. "You are not your resume or your stat sheet," she emphasizes. "You are a whole person with inherent worth."

Another key reflection for Venus is about vulnerability and strength. Early in life, she equated strength with never showing weakness. This belief was reinforced in sports, where she was praised for playing through pain and dominating opponents with unflinching will. However, when she faced depression, she discovered that real strength sometimes means admitting you need help.

It took more courage to say, "I am not okay," than to sink two free throws in a hostile arena. She often shares this paradox: "I became stronger when I acknowledged that I was weak." By talking with therapists, crying in front of close friends, and letting her family back in, Venus found a path to healing. Now, she holds vulnerability as a core component of strength. She especially imparts this message to young men and women who, like her younger self, might think they have to face everything alone.

Venus also explores the concept of forgiveness. Part of her healing involved forgiving those who hurt her—and forgiving herself for perceived failures and mistakes. Forgiving her abuser was incredibly difficult, and it did not mean she condoned what happened. Instead, it meant deciding not to let anger and hatred control her future.

"Holding onto anger is like drinking poison and expecting the other person to die," the saying goes, and Venus found truth in that. Likewise, she had to forgive herself—for not meeting the sky-high expectations she once set, for perceived "weakness" during her depression, for the time lost in pain. Through faith, she came to believe God had forgiven her, and she needed to extend that same grace to herself. This self-forgiveness lifted a heavy burden from her heart.

Faith is another deep well from which Venus draws meaning. She often reflects on how her spiritual faith was tested and strengthened through adversity. At her lowest, she questioned God's plan—Why me? Why this? Feeling abandoned. But after surviving those trials, she reframed her narrative: Why not me? Her hardships could serve a greater purpose. Venus believes there was meaning to her pain. It has made her an empathetic listener, an enthusiastic advocate, and someone who connects with others in their suffering.

She recalls a Bible verse that resonates deeply: "And we know that all things work together for good to those who love God, to those who are called according to His purpose." She interprets this not as a simple explanation that everything was good, it was not—but as a reminder that something good can emerge from something bad. Her life after basketball is dedicated to finding and fostering that good.

In quiet moments, Venus often writes in her journals or prays to the Lord, and those entries reveal deep gratitude. Despite everything, she is thankful for where she is now—gratitude for her son, who brings her joy. I am grateful for the chance to reach the pinnacle of sports—and for being forced to grow in new ways afterward. Gratitude for friends who never gave up on her. Gratitude for each morning, she wakes up healthy and able to make a difference. Cultivating gratitude became a healing practice, shifting her focus from what she lost to what she still has and what she can build anew.

Venus also reflects on the notion of purpose. When she asks, "Why am I here? What is my purpose now?" The answer she finds is service. She believes her purpose is to use her story to shed light on mental health, inspire resilience, and mentor the next generation. This sense of purpose gives her a reason to rise each day enthusiastically. It is why she continues to speak out, coach, and write.

The purpose she discovered is not fixed. Another can emerge when one purpose, like being an athlete—is fulfilled or cut short. Life has many chapters, each with its own mission. Venus's life after basketball became about people rather than points. In that, she found a purpose that, in her words, "fills my heart more than any championship ever could."

Lastly, Venus speaks of hope. In the darkest nights of her soul, she nearly lost hope altogether. Regaining it was a slow, painstaking process, but now it has become an unbreakable thread woven through her life. She wants anyone who hears her story to leave with hope. She often says, "If I can come back from where I was, anyone can. There is always hope." And she truly believes it. This hope is not naive optimism; it is hope forged in suffering, tempered by reality, and proven by her resurrection from despair. It's the kind of hope that acknowledges life's hardships but insists tomorrow can be better.

In summary, the "deeper" aspects of Venus Lacy's journey reveal lessons about identity beyond one's profession, the strength found in vulnerability, the necessity of forgiveness, the power of faith, the practice of gratitude, discovering renewed purpose, and the importance of holding onto hope. These reflections allow Venus's story to resonate with people from all walks of life, not just sports fans. They show that Venus Lacy's legacy extends beyond the points she scored to encompass the wisdom she gained and shared.

Through these insights, Venus transforms her narrative from a personal memoir into a source of guidance and inspiration, offering a beacon to countless others navigating their own life challenges.

FACTS ABOUT VENUS LACY

High school

Lacy was a star basketball player at Brainerd High School in Chattanooga, Tennessee.

In 1984, she led her team to the TSSAA state championship.

She was named Miss Basketball in her senior year.

College

Lacy played basketball at Louisiana Tech University.

In 1988, she led the Lady Techsters to the NCAA Women's Division I Basketball Championship.

1990, she was a consensus Kodak All-American and the WBCA Player of the Year.

Professional

Played professionally in Japan, Italy, and Greece.

In 1996, she was the first player selected in the American Basketball League (ABL) Draft.

In 1999, she played for the New York Liberty in the WNBA.

Olympic

In 1996, Lacy won a gold medal with the U.S. women's basketball team at the Atlanta Olympics.

Other

Lacy was inducted into the Louisiana Tech University Athletic Hall of Fame in 2011.

In 2014, she was inducted into the Louisiana Sports Hall of Fame.

Venus Lacy Parkway in Chattanooga is named in her honor.

In 2022, the Chattanooga African American Museum paid homage to Venus Lacy and many others.

In 2025, Girls Inc. of Chattanooga honored Venus Lacy.

FROM VENUS LACY

What I have come to understand is that mental health issues affect everyone, and we must work toward a society where individuals can feel safe—free to discuss their struggles without judgment. A society where not only athletes but a collective sense of optimism supports everyone.

I am fortunate to be surrounded by people who embody a spirit of service and positivity. When I speak with young audiences, I strongly emphasize that they deserve love and respect. There should be no shame in seeking help—something I wish I had learned sooner. While striving for peak performance is commendable, prioritizing your overall well-being and happiness is far more important.

For a long time, I felt I had to be the best and accept everything just to be accepted by others. I was driven by need, not by the Holy Spirit—unaware that God gave me a gift and made me "special" in His eyes. I did not understand my true worth and the freedom to be myself.

PUBLIC EYE

Living in the public eye can be tough. When you win, it's all cheers and applause. But when you slip up, the scrutiny is immediate, overwhelming, and impossible to escape. In sports and entertainment, the pressure is often compounded by critics who focus solely on performance. That's why mental strength is just as crucial as physical strength in the game. This is the reality of life under the spotlight.

In women's sports especially, the nonstop commentary from critics only adds to the pressure. It's a reminder that mental resilience is just as important as physical strength. We must have honest conversations about what happens after the playing days are over—before it's too late. It only takes one moment, one story, to change a life.

Mental health is real. Athletes are real people. So, let's talk about it, make changes, and finally break the stigma around mental health.

If you or someone you know is faced with a mental health crisis, call the crisis hotline of the local mental health or local behavioral health authority for your county.

Crisis services are available 24/7 and include a prompt face-to-face crisis assessment.

ENCOURAGEMENT

You cannot successfully reposition yourself without the support, encouragement, and commitment of those around you. Your circle should include people who share your vision and truly understand who you are. Likewise, any significant endeavor becomes possible through the collective efforts of those who believe in—and contribute to—its purpose.

Put God first in your life and follow His principles, and He will lead you to places beyond what you can imagine!

Looking for Inspiration, Motivation, or Coaching

Tap N Coaching TR

www.tap-n-coaching.com

Coach T

ATHLETES OVERCOMING

The topic of mental health—especially in the context of athletes—is one Venus Lacy addresses with deep passion and empathy. Having endured her own mental health struggles, she has become a vocal advocate for greater awareness and support for those performing under intense pressure. In this section, we explore the landscape of athlete mental health through Venus's personal journey and the broader lens of current research, shedding light on depression, its impact, and the path to recovery.

For much of her early life and career, mental health was not something Venus gave much thought to. Like many athletes, she was trained to focus on physical strength and mental toughness, often equated with suppressing feelings of anxiety, fear, or sadness.

The culture of sports, especially decades ago, left little space for open conversations about depression or emotional burnout. In Venus's era, struggling internally meant you were expected to "shake it off" or "play through it," just like a sprained ankle. Acknowledging mental strain was often seen as a sign of weakness—and that stigma ran deep.

This shift in awareness began for Venus when she encountered clinical depression following the career-altering car accident and her eventual retirement from basketball. Depression is more than just feeling sad—it's a medical condition that drains energy, clouds thinking, and makes even the most routine tasks feel overwhelming. Venus describes her depression as a "heavy fog" that settled over her life. She felt deep emptiness and despair that she simply wished would go away. At her lowest point, as previously recounted, she experienced suicidal thoughts.

During the depths of her depression, Venus also noticed physical symptoms, including extreme fatigue, significant weight gain, and memory problems—she has shared that she experienced memory loss around the time of her accident and the ensuing depression. She struggled with insomnia some nights and overslept on others, unable to find any sense of balance. These are hallmark symptoms of major depression: shifts in appetite and weight, sleep disturbances, cognitive slowing, and overwhelming sadness or irritability. It's important to understand that mental health struggles often manifest physically, something that can be especially confusing for athletes, who are trained to focus on physical signs. Venus recalled thinking, "Is something wrong with my body?"—before realizing it was her mind crying out for help.

Today, Venus actively spreads a clear message: mental health is just as important as physical health. She urges young athletes to pay attention to their emotions and seek help early. She encourages coaches and sports organizations to create environments where asking for psychological support is welcomed, not stigmatized. The world of sports, she notes, is beginning to catch up with this idea. Many teams now have mental health professionals on staff, and open discussions about stress and burnout are becoming more common.

In conclusion, this "Mental" chapter underscores that Venus Lacy's legacy goes far beyond her athletic achievements, including her vital role as a mental health advocate. Through her journey with depression and recovery, she brings visibility to an issue that remained hidden for far too long. She stands as living proof that even when an athlete stumbles in the unseen game of mental health, they can rise again with proper support and treatment. Her story is rooted in hope—demonstrating that it's possible not only to survive depression but to thrive and guide others toward healing. As Venus often reminds audiences, mental illness is not a life sentence; with help, there is always a path forward. She has walked that path and now leads others to follow.

In competitive sports, athletes are often idolized as modern-day gladiators—celebrated for their physical prowess, mental toughness, and unbreakable will.

From the outside, they appear to lead lives of glory and confidence. Yet behind many triumphant smiles lies a hidden struggle. In recent years, a growing number of elite athletes have stepped forward to break the silence around mental health challenges, revealing the truth that fans and sporting institutions are finally confronting that athletes are human beings and are not immune to depression, anxiety, or emotional turmoil.

In sports terminology, we are entering a new season where mental health is part of the game plan. The playbook is still being written, but one thing is sure: everyone wins when athletes and audiences embrace humanity behind the heroics.

And that kind of victory—measured in life improved and even saved—is more meaningful than any trophy.

ENCOURAGEMENT

(Inspiring Others to Rise Above)

As we conclude the remarkable story of Venus Lacy, it's fitting to end with a message of encouragement that reflects the spirit of hope and resilience that defines her journey. Venus often says that if her life story can help someone else find strength, then every struggle she endured was worth it. In that spirit, here are the key takeaways and words of inspiration drawn from her experiences, offered to anyone who may be facing their own challenges:

➤ **You Are Stronger Than You Know:** Venus's life proves that human potential is immense. A girl who was once told she might never walk became an Olympic champion. A woman who once felt life was no longer worth living emerged as a beacon of strength. Within you, too, lies a well of resilience that often reveals itself only in adversity. When times are hard, remember—you've survived 100% of your worst days so far, and you're still here, still fighting.

➢ **Every Setback Can Be a Setup for a Comeback**: Venus faced career and life-ending setbacks. Yet each time, she found a way to rise again, sometimes in a new form, often stronger and wiser. If you've hit a roadblock or stumbled, view it as a chapter, not the end of your story. The comeback is often the most potent part of a legacy.

➢ **Do Not Be Afraid to Ask for Help**: One of the bravest things Venus ever did was say, "I need help." Whether it was leaning on her coaches to sharpen her game or turning to mental health professionals to heal her mind, she learned that accepting support is not a sign of weakness. You don't have to carry your burdens alone. People—friends, family, counselors, support groups—are ready to help. Don't hesitate to reach out. Asking for help is an act of courage and self-care.

- ➤ **Believe in Yourself When Others Doubt You (and Even When You Doubt Yourself):** Venus was doubted at many turns—doctors questioned her ability to walk, recruiters initially overlooked her, and critics dismissed her. But her greatest doubter became herself during her battle with depression. Overcoming those doubts began with small sparks of self-belief, often ignited by someone else's faith in her—like her mother's or her coach's. Surround yourself with people who believe in you, and let their beliefs strengthen your own. Affirm yourself that you are capable and worthy, even if it means saying it every day in the mirror until you finally believe it.

- ➤ **Use Your Pain to Fuel Your Purpose:** Venus turned her pain into a mission to uplift others—and you can, too. Some of the world's most powerful contributions come from people who transformed hardship into empathy and purpose. Whatever you've been through, it has equipped you to understand and help someone else who is struggling. Pain has meaning when we use it to light someone else's path.

➢ **Stay Grounded in Your Values:** Throughout every hardship, Venus returned to the core values instilled in her—faith, kindness, perseverance, and gratitude. When life grew chaotic, those values served as her compass. Identify what matters most to you and let those values guide your decisions and reactions. They will keep you anchored, even when the world around you feels unsteady.

➢ **Celebrate Small Victories:** Venus's journey reminds us that while significant victories—titles, medals—are incredible, small wins truly pave the path forward. Her first steps without braces, her first basket in ninth grade, and her first honest conversation about depression were small victories that led to larger triumphs. No matter where you are on your journey, find something to be proud of each day, no matter how modest. Progress is progress.

➢ **Never Underestimate the Power of Hope:** There were moments when Venus felt hopeless, but hope kept flickering—sustained by faith, family, and a faint vision of a better tomorrow. Hope is a powerful lifeline. Even if it feels like just a glimmer, hold onto it. Fan it gently into a flame by imagining the future you want and taking one step at a time toward it. If you have hope, you have a reason to keep going.

Venus Lacy's story is a testament to the indomitable human spirit. She has shown us that "wins do not define a champion, but by how they recover when they fall." In her life—as in basketball, sometimes you miss the shot or get knocked down. But you can get back up, steal the ball, and score again.

If you have further questions, contact us at Stallworth INC. Our regular business hours are Mon-Fri. 9:30 am – 5 pm CST. During these hours, you can reach us by phone or email. Outside these hours, either call and leave a message or email us. We are here to help!

Email: lgentertainment2010@gmail.com

PO BOX 841121

Pearland, TX 77584

Venus Lacy: Being Different is a powerful biography chronicling the extraordinary life of Olympic gold medalist and basketball legend Venus Lacy. Written by LaQuan "LQ" Stallworth, the book goes beyond sports to reveal a profound journey of resilience, adversity, and redemption. Venus's story is a testament to perseverance and the power of the human spirit, from being born with a severe knee condition and told she might never walk to standing tall on the Olympic podium.

Raised in Chattanooga, Tennessee, in a strict and often turbulent household, Venus faced bullying, poverty, and domestic trauma. Her path to greatness began when she discovered basketball in junior high—a game that became a sanctuary and springboard for change. Despite early setbacks, including a difficult start at Old Dominion University, Venus transferred to Louisiana Tech, where she flourished— emerging as a dominant force and helping her team secure a national championship.

Her professional career took her overseas before she joined the American Basketball League and, eventually, the WNBA. However, a devastating car accident and subsequent mental health struggles led to a painful and dramatic fall. The story takes a raw, emotional turn as Venus confronts battles with depression, abuse, isolation, and suicidal thoughts.

Yet through faith, therapy, and the transformative experience of motherhood, Venus finds a new sense of purpose. The birth of her son and the support of loved ones help her reclaim her voice and rebuild her life. Today, she uses her platform to advocate for mental health awareness, mentor young athletes, and inspire others to embrace what makes them unique.

More than an athlete, Venus Lacy: Being Different is a deeply human story of survival, strength, and the courage to keep moving forward. It's a tribute to those who rise from darkness to find the light—not just on the court, but within themselves.

AUTHOR

LAQUAN "LQ" STALLWORTH

LaQuan Stallworth is a distinguished former professional basketball player who is celebrated for her dynamic career in the U.S. and abroad. Her journey began in Silsbee, Texas. LaQuan's great accomplishments led her to be inducted into the Texas Basketball Hall of Fame.

Beyond her accomplishments on the court, Stallworth has also made her mark in the creative arts as a filmmaker and author. She co-wrote the book Finding My Lost Soul and wrote and directed the films Caught Between the Two (2016) and Sins of a Scorned Wife (2020), showcasing her storytelling talent and visionary creativity. In recognition of her impact on and off the court, she has cemented her legacy as a multifaceted professional who has excelled not only in sports but also in business and mentorship.

Venus Lacy

1996 OLYMPIC GOLD MEDALIST